BRANCH LINES AROUND LYDNEY

Vic Mitchell and Keith Smith

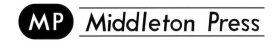

MP Middleton Press

Front cover: A Berkeley Road train was recorded at Lydney Town on 4th June 1960, with 0-4-2T no. 1431 in charge. (R.S.Carpenter)

Rear cover: Railway restoration is seen at its best as 2-6-2T no. 5541 waits to work the 15.25 Dean Forest Railway service from Lydney to Norchard on 26th May 2001. (P.G.Barnes)

Published April 2008

ISBN 978 1 906008 26 0

© Middleton Press, 2008

Design Deborah Esher
Typesetting Barbara Mitchell

Published by
      Middleton Press
      Easebourne Lane
      Midhurst
      West Sussex
      GU29 9AZ
Tel: 01730 813169
Fax: 01730 812601
Email: info@middletonpress.co.uk
www.middletonpress.co.uk

Printed & bound by Biddles Ltd, Kings Lynn

BRANCHES

INDEX

I. Route plan in 1900 with earlier ownerships. (Railway Magazine)

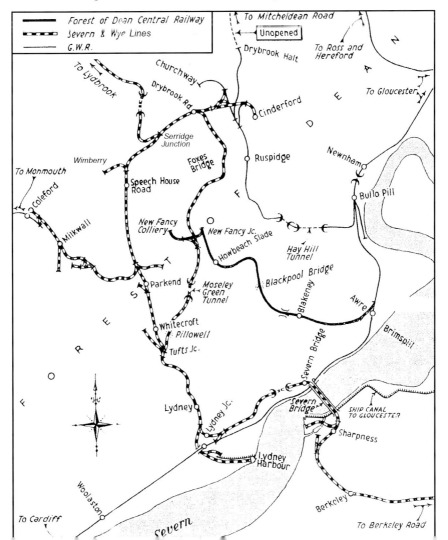

ACKNOWLEDGEMENTS

We are very grateful for the assistance received from many of those mentioned in the credits also to A.R.Carder, R.Caston, L.Crosier, G.Croughton, N.Langridge, B.Lewis, J.S.Metherall, Mr D. and Dr. S.Salter and in particular, our always supportive wives, Barbara Mitchell and Janet Smith.

GEOGRAPHICAL SETTING

Our journey starts on the southern slope of the valley of the River Severn in Gloucestershire. The route descends to Sharpness Docks, which were built at the western end of the canal to Gloucester.

It passed over the Severn on a series of bridge spans to the north bank and then parallel to it to reach Lydney, which had its own docks. These were only suitable for small vessels.

The remainder of the lines are on the high ground of the Forest of Dean under which there are bowl-like strata of coal, which have been worked for centuries, but now yield little. There are also useful layers of limestone and iron deposits. In addition to timber, the forest products have included much charcoal and associated chemicals. Coal, in particular, generated a great deal of rail traffic in the past.

The other important river is the Wye, which the railway reached at Lydbrook. The other towns of note are Coleford and Cinderford, which are respectively on the western and eastern flanks of the upland mass. The area was involved in working the iron deposits in both foundries and colour works.

The maps are to the scale of 25ins to 1 mile, with north at the top, unless otherwise indicated.

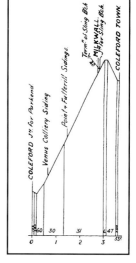

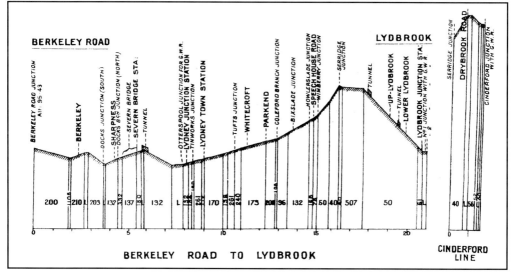

BERKELEY ROAD TO LYDBROOK

CINDERFORD LINE

HISTORICAL BACKGROUND

The story of the main part of the route goes back to the Monmouth Tramroad and to the Lydney & Lidbrook (sic) Railway's Act of 1809, which authorised a 3ft 6ins horse-worked tramroad for mineral traffic. It had no stock and charged tolls to its users; there were eight branches. It opened in June 1810 and the name was changed to the Severn & Wye Railway and Canal Company.

The first long distance line in the district was the 7ft 0¼ins gauge South Wales Railway, which ran between Gloucester and Chepstow (East) from 1851. It opened a goods branch north to the Cinderford area in 1854 and became part of the Great Western Railway in 1863.

The S&WR began to use locomotives in October 1864 and increased its track gauge to that of the GWR in 1869. However, it had to change again in 1872, when the main line was narrowed to standard gauge.

There were two Acts of local importance in July 1872. The S&WR was empowered to build a mineral branch to Coleford and the Severn Bridge Railway was authorised to construct a line from Lydney to Sharpness, where new and larger docks would facilitate the shipping of coal.

The Ross & Monmouth Railway opened in 1873 and was operated as part of the GWR. The S&WR connected with it at Lydbrook Junction on 26th August 1874; passenger services south to Lydney began on 23rd September 1875. Coleford received such trains from 9th December 1875. (It had GWR trains from Monmouth from September 1883). Drybrook Road was the first station provided for Cinderford. The complex details of the evolution of services in this area are given in that section.

Trains began carrying passengers over the Severn on 17th October 1879, the S&WR and the SBR having just merged. The Midland Railway had opened a branch from its 1844 Gloucester-Bristol main line for goods on 2nd August 1875. It ran from Berkeley Road to Sharpness and carried passengers from 1st August 1876.

By 1888, the S&WR had 13 locomotives, plus the bad luck of the recent opening of the Severn Tunnel to compete with its bridge. Financial problems resulted in the company being vested jointly in the GWR and MR on 1st July 1894, along with the MR's branch to Sharpness.

The MR became part of the London Midland & Scottish Railway in 1923, but the joint committee continued. It withdrew passenger services from the Coleford branch on 8th June 1929 and from the Lydney Town - Cinderford - Lydbrook Junction sections on 8th July of that year.

Nationalisation in 1948 brought the LMS in the area into the London Midland Region of British Railways and the GWR became the Western Region. The lines in this volume were transferred to the WR on 1st January 1948.

All services between Lydney Town and Sharpness were withdrawn on 26th October 1960, following severe damage to the Severn Bridge. Passenger trains continued on the branch between Berkeley Road and Sharpness until 2nd November 1964.

Details of freight withdrawals are given in the captions, but we note here that the final section to close was between Lydney and Parkend, in 1976. It was this part which was the subject of a preservation scheme and has been restored by the Dean Forest Railway in stages.

More information is given later in this album on this difficult and commendable scheme. Although the Society started in 1970 and first operated at Norchard in 1978, it was to be 1986 before passengers could travel ¾ mile to the outskirts of Lydney. Services were extended to St. Mary's Halt in August 1991 and the final ½ mile was acquired in 1994. Passenger services to Lydney Junction began on 2nd June 1995.

PASSENGER SERVICES

The initial timetables provided three trains from Lydney to Lydbrook, plus one to Parkend only. There was another between Drybrook Road and Lydbrook Junction and two between Lydney and Coleford, plus two on the branch only. We find no evidence of Sunday trains.

Rationalisation soon followed and within three years the service from Lydney was down to one to Lydbrook Junction and two to Bilson Platform. The branch had three trains.

The first timetable featuring the Severn Bridge showed seven down trains from Berkeley Road: two to Lydbrook Junction, one to Cinderford and four to Lydney Junction. Three trips were provided on the Coleford branch.

Most stations were receiving at least five trains by 1910, with up to eight across the bridge. These figures had dropped to four and six after World War I.

The major cutback of services north of Lydney in 1929 left eight trains over the bridge, but within ten years this was down to five. There were eight around 1950, six in 1956 and only five at the end. These figures exclude short workings between Lydney Junction and Town stations.

July 1878
July 1910

August 1940

June 1920

BERKELEY ROAD, LYDNEY, and LYDBROOK.—Severn and Wye—Great Western and Midland.

Week Days only.

Miles		mrn	mrn	mrn	aft	aft	aft	aft	aft (Saturdays only.)	aft
	456 Bristol (Temple Meads) dep.	....	7 10	1032	....	....	2 35	4 50	....	6 37
	454 Gloucester (Mid.) ...... "	....	7 48	1055	....	1 50	3 35	5 42	....	....
—	**Berkeley Road** .... dep.	....	8 50	1150	....	2 45	4 9	6 35	....	7 33
2¼	Berkeley	....	8 56	1156	....	2 51	4 15	6 41	....	7 38
4	**Sharpness**	....	9 2	12 2	....	2 57	4 21	6 47	....	7 43
5¼	Severn Bridge, for Blakeney	....	9 7	12 7	....	3 6	4 26	6 54	....	7 48
8	**Lydney Junction 52, 53** ... arr.	....	9 15	1214	....	3 13	4 33	7 1	....	7 55
33	52 Newport .... arr.	....	1055	2 5	....	....	6 53	....	....	9 5
44¾	52 Cardiff (G. W.) .... "	....	1125	2 27	....	....	7 20	....	....	9 27
—	52 Gloucester (G. W.) ..... dep.	....	7 25	9 16	....	....	2 0	4 50	....	....
—	**Lydney** Junction .... dep.	....	9 20	1217	....	....	4 37	7 10		7 57
8¾	Lydney Town	7 20	9 25	1220	....	....	4 39	7 13		8 0
11	Whitecroft	7 27	9 32	1228	....	....	4 46	7 20		....
12¼	Parkend .... arr.	7 29	9 34	1230	....	....	4 48	7 22		....
14	Milkwall, for Clearwell	7 50	9 52	1247	....	....	5 6	7 39		....
15	**Coleford, for Staunton** ... arr.	7 54	9 56	1252	....	....	5 11	7 44		....
21	Monmouth (Troy) .... arr.	....	....	....	....	....	....	....		....
—	Parkend .... dep.	7 30	9 37	1233	....	....	4 51	7 24		....
14¼	**Speech House Road**	7 44	9 47	1242	....	....	5 1	7 35		....
17¼	**Drybrook Road**	7 53	9 54	1249	....	....	5 8	7 42		....
18½	Cinderford 54 .... arr.	7 58	9 58	1253	....	....	5 12	7 46		....
	Cinderford 54 .... dep.	8 4	10 4	....	1 48	....	5 15	....	7 55	....
—	Drybrook Road	8 8	10 8	....	1 52	....	5 19	....	7 59	....
18¾	Upper Lydbrook	8 17	1017	....	2 1	....	5 27	....	8 8	....
20½	**Lydbrook Junction 74** .... arr.	8 23	1023	....	2 7	....	....	....	8 14	....
27¼	74 Monmouth (May Hill) ... arr.	9 45	1120	....	4 0	....	....	....	....	....

Week Days only.

Miles		mrn	mrn	mrn	mrn	aft	aft	aft	aft	aft	aft	aft	aft (Except Saturdays.)	aft (Saturdays only.)
	74 Monmouth (May Hill) .... dep.	....	....	....	....	....	....	1220	....	....	3 35	....	....	7 16
—	**Lydbrook Junction** .... dep.	....	8 40	....	....	....	....	1 25	....	....	4 0	....	....	8 25
1¾	Upper Lydbrook	....	8 46	....	....	....	....	1 31	....	....	4 6	5 50	....	8 31
5¼	Drybrook Road	....	8 55	....	....	....	....	1 40	....	....	Sig.	6 0	....	8 40
6½	Cinderford 54 .... arr.	....	8 59	....	....	....	....	1 44	....	....	4 20	6 4	....	8 44
	Cinderford 54 .... dep.	....	9 2	....	....	....	1 20	....	....	....	4 23	6 7	7 55	8 50
—	Drybrook Road	....	9 6	....	....	....	1 24	....	....	....	4 27	6 11	7 59	8 54
6¾	Speech House Road	....	9 13	....	....	....	1 31	....	....	....	4 34	6 18	8 6	9 1
8½	Parkend .... arr.	....	9 24	....	....	....	1 39	....	....	....	4 43	6 29	8 16	9 11
—	Monmouth (Troy) .... dep.	....	....	....	....	....	....	....	....	....	....	....	....	....
—	Coleford .... dep.	....	8 57	....	....	1215	....	....	....	4 7	....	6 0	7 50	8 45
—	Milkwall, for Clearwell	....	9 1	....	....	1219	....	....	....	4 11	....	6 4	7 54	8 49
—	Parkend .... dep.	....	9 28	....	....	1237	1 41	....	....	4 26	4 44	6 30	8 17	9 12
9¼	Whitecroft	....	9 31	....	....	1240	1 44	....	....	4 28	4 47	6 33	8 20	9 15
11¾	Lydney Town	7 5	9 39	1035	1055	1248	1 52	....	2 55	4 37	4 55	6 41	8 28	9 23
12¼	**Lydney Junction 52, 53** .... arr.	7 7	9 41	1037	1057	1250	1 54	....	2 57	4 39	4 57	6 43	....	....
31½	53 Gloucester (G. W.) ...... arr.	8 38	1133	1133	....	2 6	3 54	....	3 54	5 29	6 45	7 43		
—	53 Cardiff (G. W.) .... dep.	....	....	....	9 10	....	12 5	....	....	....	3 50	4 30		
—	53 Newport .... "	....	....	....	9 40	....	1230	....	....	....	4 12	5 5		
—	**Lydney** Junction .... dep.	7 8	....	....	1059	....	1 56	....	2 58	....	5 5	6 46		
15½	Severn Bridge, for Blakeney	7 15	....	....	11 6	....	2 3	....	3 5	....	5 12	6 54		
16½	**Sharpness**	7 22	....	....	1111	....	2 9	....	3 11	....	5 18	7 0		
18½	Berkeley	7 28	....	....	1117	....	2 15	....	3 17	....	5 26	7 7		
20½	**Berkeley Road, 454, 456** ... arr.	7 34	....	....	1123	....	2 21	....	3 22	....	5 32	7 13		
35½	456 Gloucester (Mid.) ...... arr.	8 10	....	....	1213	....	....	....	4 18	....	6 46	8 3		
42½	454 Bristol (Temple Meads). "	9 53	....	....	1240	....	3 38	....	4 45	....	7 30	8 55		

BERKELEY ROAD and LYDNEY TOWN

WEEK DAYS ONLY—(Second class only)

Miles		am	am	am	pm E	pm S	pm S	pm S	pm E	pm	pm S
	Berkeley Road .. dep	8 22	..	1152	1 40	2 10	..	4 50	5 10	6 28	..
2¼	Berkeley	8 28	....	1158	1 45	2 15	....	4 55	5 16	6 34	....
4¼	Sharpness	8 34	..	12 4	1 52	2 22	..	5 1	5 22	6 40	..
5½	Severn Bridge for Blakeney	8 39	....	12 9	1 56	2 26	....	5 6	5 27	6 45	....
8¼	Lydney Junction .. arr	8 46	..	1216	2 4	2 34	..	5 14	5 34	6 52	..
	Lydney Junction .. dep	8 49	1015	1219	2 7	2 37	4 55	5 16	5 37	6 55	7 15
9	**Lydney Town** .. arr	8 51	1018	1221	2 9	2 39	4 57	5 19	5 39	6 57	7 18

Miles		am	am	am	pm E	pm S	pm S	pm E	pm S	pm
	Lydney Town .. dep	7 10	9 55	1050	1 5	1 10	3 55	4 25	4 45	5 44
¾	Lydney Junction .. arr	7 12	9 58	1052	1 7	1 12	3 57	4 27	4 47	5 46
	Lydney Junction .. dep	7 13	..	1053	1 8	1 13	3 58	4 28	..	5 47
3½	Severn Bridge for Blakeney	7 20	....	11 0	1 15	1 20	4 5	4 35	....	5 54
4¾	Sharpness	7 25	..	11 5	1 20	1 25	4 10	4 40	..	5 59
6¾	Berkeley	7 30	....	1110	1 26	1 31	4 16	4 46	....	6 5
9	**Berkeley Road** .. arr	7 36	..	1116	1 31	1 36	4 21	4 51	..	6 10

E Except Saturdays S Saturdays only

August 1960

BERKELEY ROAD

II.   The 1930 map at 2ins to 1 mile has the station on the right, along with the triangular junction. The west-south section of it was open between 1908 and 1963, but carried no regular passenger service.

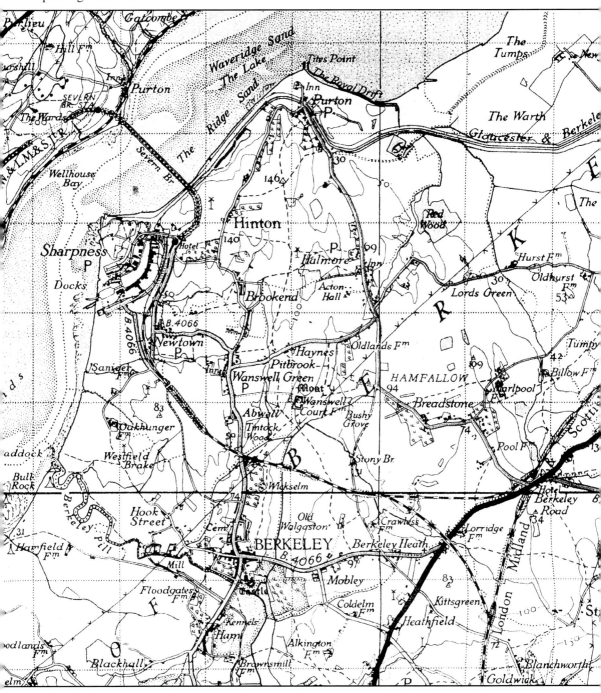

1.	The main line to Bristol is on the left of this photograph from 1947. The branch train is formed of GWR stock; MR coaches were used until 1929. The branch was singled beyond the bridge on 26th July 1931. (Stations UK)

2.	A closer view of the branch platforms on the same day includes a horse box in the dock. All passenger service ceased at this station on 4th January 1965, but freight continued until 1st November 1966. More recently, the branch has been authorised for overnight stops of the Royal Train. (Stations UK)

III.	The 1921 map has the MR main line from Gloucester to Bristol from top to bottom. On the left is the 1875 branch to Sharpness. The station opened in 1844 and was named "Dursley and Berkeley" for its first year.

3.　　　The means of crossing the main lines is seen in the previous pictures; in the foreground is the provision for the branch. No. 2080 is about to pass over it on 14th September 1951 with the 6.35pm to Lydney Town. The platform on the right was not used by passenger trains in the final years. (R.M.Casserley)

Other views can be seen in pictures
numbered 68 to 72 in our
Gloucester to Bristol album.
The triangular junction is also described therein.

4. A northward panorama from 27th June 1954 includes the signal box and part of the goods yard. The building was added in 1876 when the branch opened for passengers. (Lens of Sutton coll.)

5. The east elevations of both buildings were recorded on the same day. The nearest one was to Brunel's design, with an all-round awning, but this feature did not last to the end. All structures were lost in about 1965, except the station house. (Lens of Sutton coll.)

BERKELEY

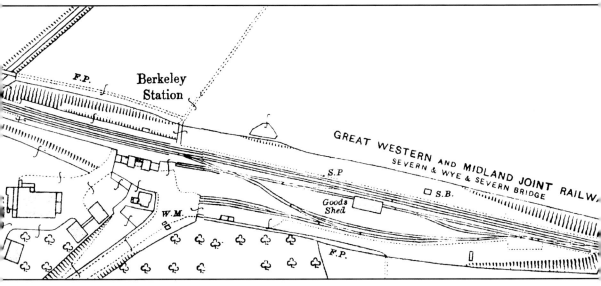

IV.   The 1921 edition does not include the short tramway that ran across the station approach in 1917-21 to serve the large building on the left, which was a dairy. The signal box is shown as S.B. and it closed in 1931. The route was regularly used by trains between London and South Wales, diverted due to work in the Severn Tunnel, usually on Sundays.

6.   This peaceful panorama is from 1959, when all was well kept. Sadly everything was destroyed following withdrawal of passenger service in 1964. The village had a population of 774 in 1901. (R.M.Casserley)

7.   A Lydney Town to Berkeley Road service was recorded in January 1960, hauled by 0-6-0PT no. 1643. In the background is the goods yard, which was in use until 1st November 1966. The shed (left) housed a 30cwt crane. (M.A.N.Johnston)

8.   A gantry crane was erected for the transfer of nuclear waste flasks, but the facility has been used irregularly. For example, there was a Wednesdays-only 12.40 departure for Crewe, but it ran only once in the last four months of 2007. Berkeley power station was productive in 1962-89 and most subsequent traffic has come from Oldbury power station. Nos 20306 and 20312 were recorded on 15th September 2004. (B.J.Ashworth)

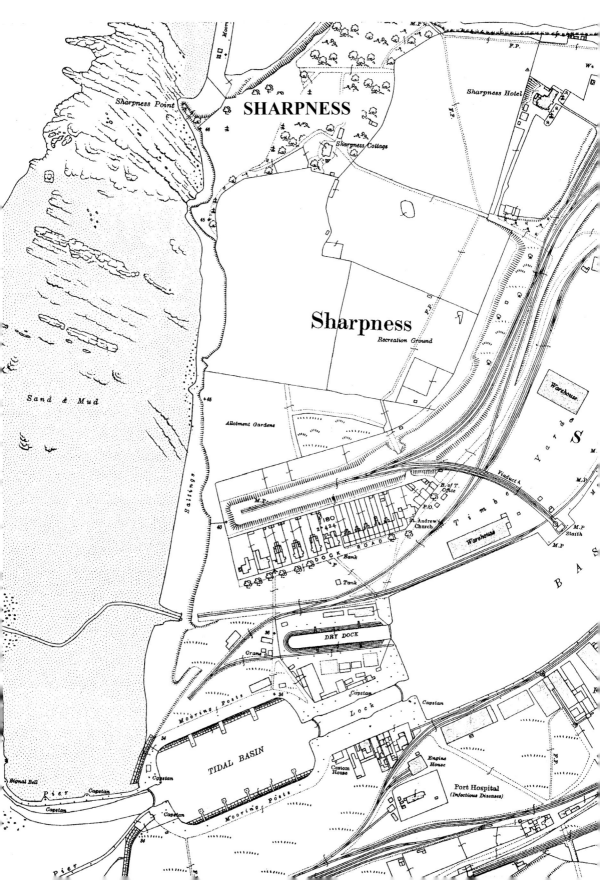

SHARPNESS

Sharpness Point

Sharpness Hotel

Sharpness Cottage

Sharpness

Recreation Ground

Sand & Mud

Allotment Gardens

Saltings

Warehouse

Yards

S

B. of T.
Office

M.P.

180
2 424

St. Andrew's
Church

P.O.

Timber

DOCK   ROAD

Bank

Tank

Warehouse

M.P

Staith

M.P

BAS

DRY DOCK

Crane

Capstan

Mooring Posts

Capstan

Lock

Engine
House

Viaduct

Custom
House

Port Hospital
(Infectious Diseases)

Signal Bell

Pier   Capstan

Capstan

TIDAL BASIN

Capstan

Mooring Posts

Pier

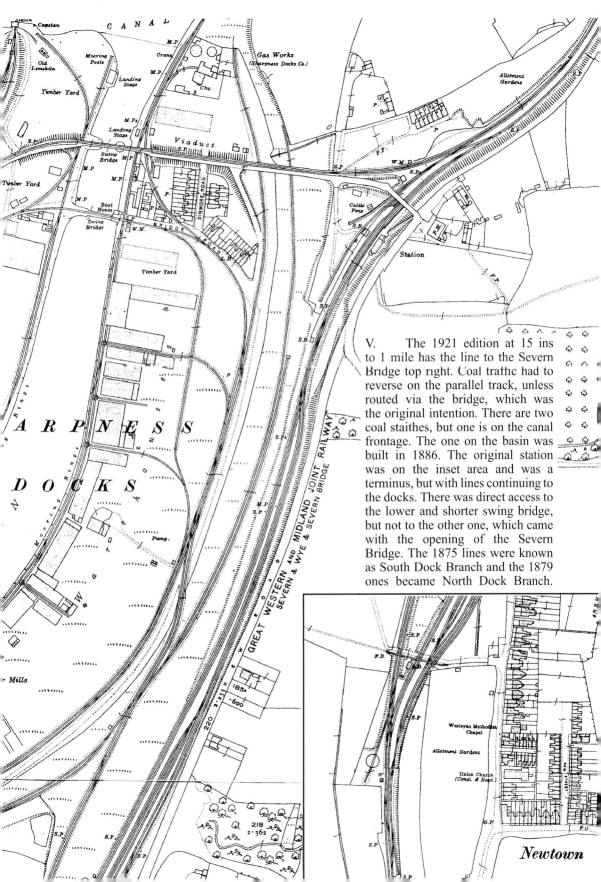

V.   The 1921 edition at 15 ins to 1 mile has the line to the Severn Bridge top right. Coal traffic had to reverse on the parallel track, unless routed via the bridge, which was the original intention. There are two coal staithes, but one is on the canal frontage. The one on the basin was built in 1886. The original station was on the inset area and was a terminus, but with lines continuing to the docks. There was direct access to the lower and shorter swing bridge, but not to the other one, which came with the opening of the Severn Bridge. The 1875 lines were known as South Dock Branch and the 1879 ones became North Dock Branch.

CANAL

Gas Works
(Sharpness Docks Co.)

Old Limekiln

Timber Yard

Mooring Posts

Landing Stage

Crane

Chy.

M.P.

Allotment Gardens

Landing Stage

Viaduct

Swing Bridge

Boat House

Swing Bridge

Timber Yard

Timber Yard

W.M.

Cattle Pens

Station

S.B.

SHARPNESS DOCKS

GREAT WESTERN AND MIDLAND JOINT RAILWAY

SEVERN & WYE & SEVERN BRIDGE RAILWAY

Pump.

Mills

185·600

220·2·13½

218 2·362

Wesleyan Methodist Chapel

Allotment Gardens

Union Church (Congl. & Bapt.)

Newtown

9.   A southward panorama from the road bridge has the dock area on the right. This had earlier been marshland; the ground rises on the left. Public goods traffic was handled in the yard in the right foreground until 1st November 1966. (R.S.Carpenter coll.)

10.   A 1949 photograph includes the steps to the road between the two arches. The goods yard sidings pass under the left one. (R.S.Carpenter coll.)

11.   The Birmingham Locomotive Club hired railcar no. 7, seen in this and the next picture on 27th July 1950. Sharpness South was where the South Dock Branch diverged from the station tracks and is on the inset part of the map. This is the site of the first station. The signal box was in use from 1914 to 1965. (R.S.Carpenter coll.)

12.   Evident here is the unusual attachment of a waiting shelter to a signal box. The latter functioned from 1903 until 27th October 1957. Its frame had 33 levers. (R.S.Carpenter coll.)

13. The track north from South Junction was singled in September 1956. This picture from July 1959 includes the MR fencing alongside the inclined footway. The platform on the right had lost its track in 1956. (H.C.Casserley)

14. A photograph from the penultimate year of passenger operation includes the disused cattle dock and the damaged Severn Bridge. No. 6437 is taking water before returning to Berkeley Road at 6.0pm on 17th May 1963. (B.J.Ashworth)

SHARPNESS DOCKS

15.	This is the swing bridge on North Docks Branch and is seen from the other swing bridge, with the Severn Bridge in the background. The dock joins the canal in the background. (I.A.Pope coll.)

16.	The lock is on the extreme left and beyond it are several ships moored abreast, awaiting access to the quayside in about 1930. The cylinder contained drinking water for the ships. The area passed to the British Waterways Board from the Gloucester & Sharpness Canal & Docks Company upon nationalisation in 1948. (R.H.Marrows coll.)

17.   Further north along the dock was the massive coal staithe, many times larger than those at Lydney Docks, seen later in this volume. It was the destination of the countless coal trains that crossed the Severn Bridge and the bridge in the background. The hydraulic coal tip was completed in 1908 and the white grain silo dates from 1938. (R.H.Marrows coll.)

18.   The South Dock Branch swing bridge is being approached by one of the Dock's own locomotives in 1960. The later swing bridge was at a higher level; it has since been dismantled. The cranes date from the early 1940s. (Dr. G.B.Sutton)

19.	At work in 1959 were 0-6-0PT no. 1623 and Peckett 0-4-0ST no. 2060 of 1944, a Dock locomotive. (M.A.N.Johnston)

20.	A busy scene was recorded in March 2000, but rail traffic had dwindled and vanished in the 1990s. There was hope in the next decade that there would be a revival. Shipping was buoyant, with 430 movements in 2003 for example. The docks were operated then by the Victoria Group. A railtour reached the Network Rail boundary (near picture 11) on 22nd April 2007. This is the 1873 bridge and it was still hand cranked. (R.H.Marrows)

21.   The Severn Bridge was almost ¾ mile in length and comprised 22 spans. The swinging span was over the canal and was designed for two tracks, but only ever had one. The box was manned by an engine driver and a signalman. There were only seven levers. (R.S.Carpenter coll.)

22.   The canal level was usually much higher than that of the river; the latter could vary 30ft. in 2½ hours. The chimneys are above each boiler, but only one was in steam at a time. This view is from 29th October 1960 and was taken just before completion of years of work to upgrade the structure. (M.A.N.Johnston)

23.   Two loaded petrol tankers collided with one of the piers in fog on the night of 25th October 1960 and exploded. They were seeking the lock, but were on the wrong side of the river, out of control. Five crew members died in the fire, two spans were lost and others were deformed beyond repair. Men strengthening the bridge were having a meal break at that time. During temporary support work (seen here in May 1961), a barge overturned with all lives lost and it then caused further damage to the bridge. Demolition eventually began in the late 1960s, but an unexpected collapse brought parts down into the mud and vast loss of money to all concerned. Much of the steel was irretrievable. (H.C.Casserley)

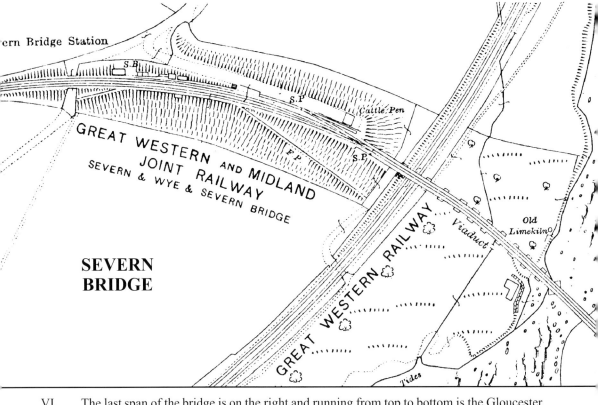

ern Bridge Station

S.B.

S.P.

Cattle Pen

GREAT WESTERN AND MIDLAND
JOINT RAILWAY
SEVERN & WYE & SEVERN BRIDGE

F.P.

S.P.

**SEVERN
BRIDGE**

GREAT WESTERN RAILWAY

Viaduct

Old
Limekiln

Tides

VI.   The last span of the bridge is on the right and running from top to bottom is the Gloucester to Chepstow line. It passes over a bridge which allowed pedestrians from the station access to the beach. This is the 1922 edition.

24.   The track was on a rising gradient of 1 in 137 from the far side of the river and trains were restricted to 15mph on the structure. The station approach road is clear in this postcard view. The main line is hidden in the trees, as are some of the 13 arches. When completed, the structure was second only to the Tay Bridge in length, at 4162ft. The original signal box is included. (I.A.Pope coll.)

25.   Two photographs from 1951 include the 1911 signal box, which had 12 levers. The short goods siding was closed on 24th June 1956 and lifted on 7th October of that year. (R.S.Carpenter coll.)

26.   The crossing was used by both passengers and the signalman. However, there were very few local residents at this windswept location. The signal box was of MR design. (R.S.Carpenter coll.)

27.   A semaphore is down on the viaduct for the passage of a short goods train behind 0-6-0PT no. 1642 on 19th July 1958. Another is up for it to pass over the points at the end of the loop, which had been lengthened in 1907. The train will soon enter Severn Bridge Tunnel, which was 506 yds long. The line was not officially closed until 1964, when bridge repair was no longer deemed to be an option. (R.E.Toop/C.G.Maggs coll.)

LM&S.&G.W. (Severn & WyeJoint) Ry.
Severn Bridge   Severn Bridge
TO
BERKELEY
THIRD   CLASS
1/01 C   Fare   1/01 C
Berkeley   Berkeley
FOR CONDITIONS SEE BACK. (R.B

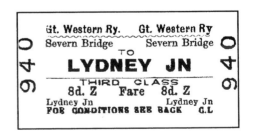

Gt. Western Ry.   Gt. Western Ry
Severn Bridge   Severn Bridge
TO
LYDNEY JN
THIRD   CLASS
8d. Z   Fare   8d. Z
Lydney Jn   Lydney Jn
FOR CONDITIONS SEE BACK   G.L

LYDNEY JUNCTION

VII. The 1930 revision is at 1½ ins to 1 mile and it shows the double track of the GWR main line lower right. Double track is also in the centre, near Whitecroft. The line passing through the D of DEAN (top right) was known as MINERAL LOOP and at that point there is a branch to New Fancy Colliery. The Coleford branch (top left) trails off the main route (top centre).

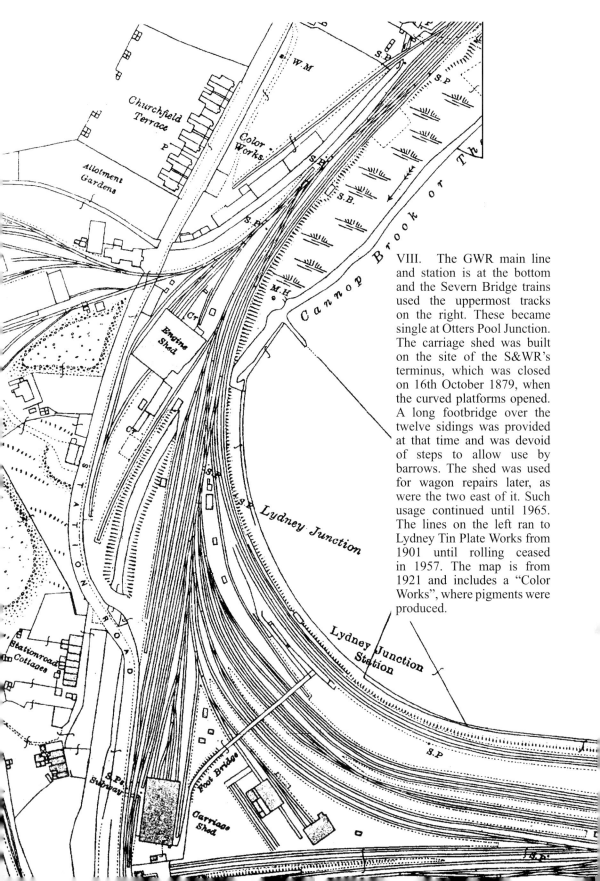

VIII. The GWR main line and station is at the bottom and the Severn Bridge trains used the uppermost tracks on the right. These became single at Otters Pool Junction. The carriage shed was built on the site of the S&WR's terminus, which was closed on 16th October 1879, when the curved platforms opened. A long footbridge over the twelve sidings was provided at that time and was devoid of steps to allow use by barrows. The shed was used for wagon repairs later, as were the two east of it. Such usage continued until 1965. The lines on the left ran to Lydney Tin Plate Works from 1901 until rolling ceased in 1957. The map is from 1921 and includes a "Color Works", where pigments were produced.

28.   This eastward panorama is from the lower left corner of the map, prior to the change from broad gauge in 1872. Under the bridge is Cannop Brook and beyond it is the level crossing. In the road is the S&WR single line and a tramroad track to Lydney Docks. Further on are a pair of shunting horses on the main line and the GWR goods shed is on the right. The station building of 1852 was of Brunel's chalet style. (I.A.Pope coll.)

29.   An eastward view has the single line from Severn Bridge in front of Otters Pool Junction box, which is on the left. The main lines are to the right of the wagons. This and the next picture were taken in 1947. (L.E.Copeland/Wild Swan Publications)

30. The north elevation of the main line station is featured, along with its access path (left), which passed under the dock lines in the subway shown on the map. There is also a foot crossing near the gates. The flat crossing of the South Wales main line by the tramway was in use until 1882. The standard gauge crossing lasted until October 1963, the dock lines having closed in August 1963. (L.E.Copeland/Wild Swan Publications)

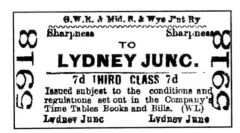

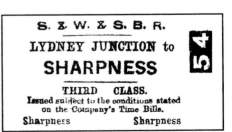

31.   Three photographs from around 1950 feature the former S&WR platforms. The term "Lydney Junction" was used on the main line from 1955 to 1968. The platform on the left has direct connection to the gently inclined footbridge, which was erected in 1908. (H.C.Casserley)

32.   An 0-6-0PT is waiting at the same platform, ready to leave for Lydney Town. The photographer is at the foot of the bridge. The fencing is typical MR style and the sign was of LMS form. (L.E.Copeland/Wild Swan Publications)

33.   The signal box was built in 1906 and was for long known as "Lydney Yard", but latterly as "S&W Yard". It had a 16-lever frame and closed on 28th June 1960. It is visible in the previous two photographs. The loco is no. 4987. (SLS coll.)

IX.   This map continues east from the previous one and it includes two signal boxes: Otters Pool Junction and Lydney Junction (left), the latter lasting until 1969. The up and down goods loops were still in place in 2008, as was a box controlling barriers at the main line level crossing.

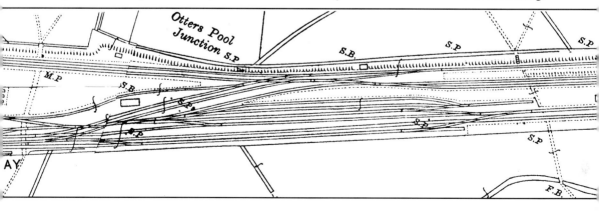

34.   A 1959 northward view shows that the docks line was parallel to the road crossing. The former closed on 25th August 1963 and was removed within weeks. (M.A.N.Johnston)

35.   No. 1623 was photographed from a main line train on 14th April 1962 whilst coupled to an ex-GWR shunters truck. Beyond the brake van can be seen the 1914 Otters Pool signal box; its 22-lever frame was in use until 14th February 1965. At the other end of the connection with the main line was Lydney Junction box, which lasted until 3rd March 1969. (B.W.L.Brooksbank)

36.   The Dean Forest Railway restored passenger service to Lydney in 1995 and 2-6-2T no. 5541 was recorded on 21st May 2001 running round its train, using the level crossing over the realigned Station Road. The signal box had been moved from Heysham Harbour. (P.G.Barnes)

37.   A new platform had to be built and an island style was chosen, although a foot crossing from the road was necessary. The connection with the up goods loop was first used by a passenger train on 22nd April 2007, when the "Severnside Rambler" arrived behind ex-LMS 4-6-0 no. 45407. No. 5541 is seen on the same day, waiting with the 15.25 to Norchard. (P.G.Barnes)

Lydney
Engine Shed

38.   The position of the box is shown top right on map VIII and it is seen backing onto marshland. The box also controlled access to the tinplate works sidings. The frame had 27 levers when taken out of use on 2nd October 1967. (R.K.Blencowe)

Other views can be found in pictures 37-46 in our
***Gloucester to Cardiff* album.**

39.   The S&WR established its engine shed here, but the buildings seen are the repair shops. Nos 7741 and 1623 are on the running shed roads on 31st August 1952. This was a sub-shed of Gloucester, then coded 85B. (M.Dart/Transport Treasury)

40.　　Inside the 1886 repair shop on 23rd June 1962 is 0-6-0PT no. 5420. The forge is on the right, but there is no evidence of powered tools. Gas lighting was provided. The buffer beam has been moved forward to give access to the cylinders. (B.J.Ashworth)

41.　　The running shed (left) was recorded in the 1950s. The store building is in the centre and the chimney on the right is part of the sand drier. Closure came on 2nd March 1964. There were usually 14 locos based here in the 1920s. (R.Dagley-Morris/I.A.Pope coll.)

LYDNEY DOCKS

42.   A 1936 panorama includes two of the coal tips on the south bank. There were four more near the lock; there had been three others beyond the barge until 1927. The line to the lock closed in 1963. The crane was rated at only two tons. (D.K.Jones coll.)

43.   The entrance to the lock is on the left in this view from September 1960. The hoists were manually operated and could only load very small ships, hence the decline of the dock in favour of Sharpness. Most coal was destined for harbours between Bristol and Ilfracombe. (M.A.N.Johnston)

Maps of the docks can be found near photographs 47 and 48 in *Gloucester to Cardiff.* The location of the harbour is shown on map VII in this volume (after picture 27).

ST. MARY'S HALT

44.   First, we have a view south with Lydney Junction in the background. This is from about 1959 with the tracks described from left to right: up, down, third line and weighbridge siding, which was actually a long loop. No. 1632 is northbound with empties. (M.A.N.Johnston)

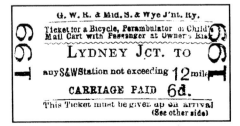

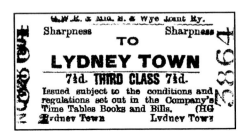

45.   St. Mary's footbridge is the background in this northward view of wagons standing on the siding to the West of England Wagon Works (1927-59). The site was earlier used for the production of pigments from local iron oxide; see map VIII. (L.E.Copeland/Wild Swan Publications)

46.   The halt was built under the footbridge and is seen from a southbound DMU in July 2005. The opening date was 8th September 1991 and it was initially called "Lakeside". One of the other lines is overgrown; it served as a run-round loop while the halt was the terminus. It remained so until 2nd June 1995. The platform came from Blaen Rhondda. (V.Mitchell)

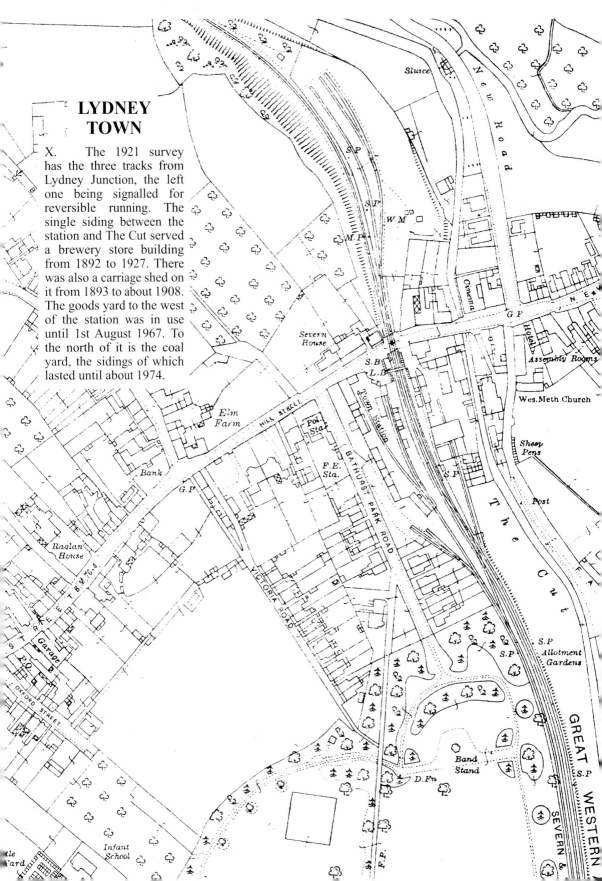

LYDNEY TOWN

X. The 1921 survey has the three tracks from Lydney Junction, the left one being signalled for reversible running. The single siding between the station and The Cut served a brewery store building from 1892 to 1927. There was also a carriage shed on it from 1893 to about 1908. The goods yard to the west of the station was in use until 1st August 1967. To the north of it is the coal yard, the sidings of which lasted until about 1974.

47.   A northward panorama includes much of the goods yard; the line on the left runs to the cattle dock. On the right are the brewery storage premises. (A.Dudman coll.)

48.   An Edwardian postcard reveals the point of platform extension. There had been a siding to a foundry on the right before the brewery store existed. The buildings on the left were completed in 1897. (M.Dart coll.)

49.   Half-cab 0-6-0PT no. 2043 is signalled for "Third Line" as it blows off on the 1 in 170 down gradient on 9th August 1947. Many of the wagons are well loaded with coal. "Third Line" had been laid on the site of the earlier tramroad, which had run behind the buildings on the left. (SLS coll.)

50.   The coal yard is in the distance as a 5400 class 0-6-0PT waits with its autotrain in the up platform on 17th August 1956. The footbridge was added in 1904. There were steps on the north side of the footbridge for the benefit of pedestrians delayed by the gates. These were worked by a wheel in the signal box. (L.E.Copeland/Wild Swan Publications)

51.   An earlier northward view from the footbridge features the commencement of the single line and also the coal yard. It seems that an old lorry was standing behind the railings between the gates. The yard had earlier been used for timber and other building materials. (L.E.Copeland/Wild Swan Publications)

52.   The signal box was downgraded to a ground frame in October 1967 and was closed in July 1969. It had a frame with 31 levers. The small gate was known as the "wicket" and people could use it until locked remotely by the signalman as the train approached. (M.Dart coll.)

53.   A photograph from 27th July 1968 reveals terminal decline but suggests that facilities were still available for ladies and gentlemen. The down line had gone in 1965. The signal box had been built in 1897. There had been sidings north hereof for Middle Forge, Upper Forge, New Mills and Kindall's Colliery. All had gone by 1906. (R.Leleux/M.J.Stretton coll.)

54.   A view towards the level crossing on 9th July 2005 features another replica building commendably created by the DFR. The new platform was further south than the original, owing to other building development, and came into use on 22nd April 2001. (V.Mitchell)

NORCHARD

XI. The 1922 issue includes the property owned by the Park Colliery Co. Ltd., which here worked the southern end of the coal basin. It used an endless rope system and had the deepest seam in the coalfield. Excessive water meant pumping out up to 3000 gallons per minute, this being equivalent to 38 tons of water for every ton of coal produced. The West Gloucester Power Co. built a power station east of the colliery, on the waste ground indicated by dots. About 50,000 tons of coal were produced per annum in the 1930s.

Air Shaft

rchard Colliery

Air Shaft

W. Ms.

Pump

GREAT WESTERN AND MIDLAND JOINT RAILWAY

SEVERN & WYE & SEVERN BRIDGE

Spring

Cannop Brook

The Lyd

S.P.

F.P.

F.P.

P

55.   The drift mine coal went up the conveyor direct into the power station, but operation of the latter ceased in 1967 and the former in 1957. The DFR acquired the heavily overgrown site in 1974 and workshops, a terminus and a car park were laid out on the level ground, centre and right. The line to Parkend climbs on the left. (I.A.Pope coll.)

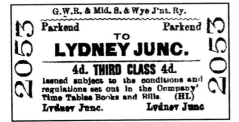

G.W.R. & Mid. S. & Wye J'nt. Ry.
2053 Parkend   TO   Parkend 2053
LYDNEY JUNC.
4d. THIRD CLASS 4d.
Issued subject to the conditions and regulations set out in the Company' Time Tables Books and Bills.   (HL)
Lydney Junc.   Lydney Junc

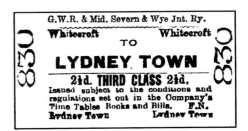

G.W.R. & Mid. Severn & Wye Jnt. Ry.
830 Whitecroft   TO   Whitecroft 830
LYDNEY TOWN
2½d. THIRD CLASS 2½d.
Issued subject to the conditions and regulations set out in the Company's Time Tables Books and Bills.   F.N.
Lydney Town   Lydney Town

56.   The DFR rolling stock was transferred from a temporary depot at Parkend on 16th January 1978 and over 10,000 visitors came that year to see the collection. Part of it stands on Kidnall's siding in the background on 24th October 1982, as no. 5541 approaches the terminus. In steam on the left is Hunslet 0-6-0ST no. 3806 of 1953. (T.Heavyside)

57.   This is the prospective passenger's perspective on 9th July 2005, with a convenient convenience of conspicuous quality on the right. Out of view to the right is the steam workshop; diesels were cared for in a temporary structure at Lydney, beyond the left edge of picture 36. The main building (left) contains a fine shop and a fascinating museum; both opened in 1989. (V.Mitchell)

58.   Passing through the building on the same day, we cross the north end of the terminal loop, while a DMU destined for Lydney waits at the low level platform. A platform at a higher level had to be provided for trains running towards Parkend. The wooden building was first used as a crossing hut near Gloucester, then at Drybrook Road, later at Cinderford (Old) and subsequently in a timber yard. (V.Mitchell)

59.   Our survey that day is completed with a view from a train arriving from the north; it is about to stop at the high level platform, which opened on 21st March 2004. In the background, stock stands on the line to the workshop. On the DFR at that time were three former GWR-owned locos, seven industrial engines, 15 ex-BR diesels and four 108 DMUs, plus 14 coaches. (V.Mitchell)

TUFTS
JUNCTION

XII. From left to right at the top we have the private Oakwood line (gated near the junction), three tracks to Whitecroft and one to the Mineral Loop. DFR DMU's ran trips this far from 18th August 2001, but passengers could not alight, Progress north was delayed by the renewal of the bridge over the brook, right centre.

Tufts
Chemical Works

Tanks

Brook

Road

Old Shaft

S.P.

Def.

S.Ps

Def.

F.P.

3 ft.Tk.H.

3 ft.R.H.

S.P.

C.S.

S.B.

F.B.

C.S.

TRAMWAY

S.Ps & R.D. Bdy.

Union & R.D. Bdy.

6 ft.B.B.

Def.

Union & R.D. Bdy.

Brook

S.P.

60.   The 1897 Tufts Junction signal box is seen in 1962. Diverging from the centre track and
passing under the gate is the Oakwood branch, which served the Lydney Chemical Company, Park
Hill Iron Mine and Colliery, Flour Mill Colliery and Princess Royal Colliery at various times. The

latter was the final user, traffic ceasing in February 1965. The box had 30 levers and was in use until 2nd October 1967. The small signal was for trains to the Mineral Loop, which was in use at its south end until June 1964. (R.Dagley-Morris/I.A.Pope coll.)

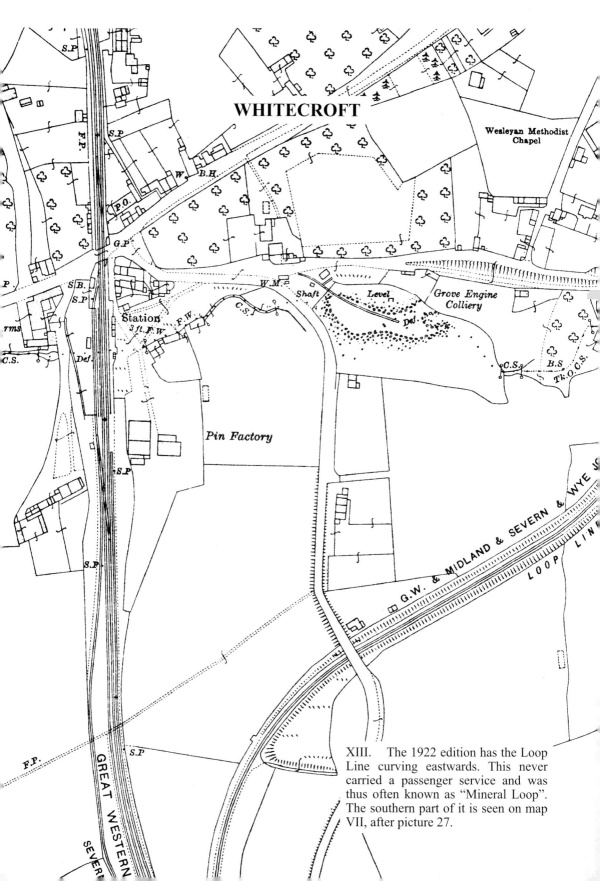

WHITECROFT

Wesleyan Methodist
Chapel

Grove Engine
Colliery

Shaft   Level

Station

Pin Factory

G.W. & MIDLAND & SEVERN & WYE J
LOOP LIN

GREAT WESTERN

SEVERN

XIII.   The 1922 edition has the Loop
Line curving eastwards. This never
carried a passenger service and was
thus often known as "Mineral Loop".
The southern part of it is seen on map
VII, after picture 27.

61.   The company's basic wooden buildings were provided here and are seen on an early postcard. The factory chimneys are on the Patent Fuel Works, which produced coal briquettes between about 1868 and 1910. Pins were the subsequent product of the premises. Its siding ran into the works and linked to a line shown on the map as a third track. This ran south to Tufts Junction until 1930, when the route was singled. It had been doubled in 1896; the third line was for freight only. (Lens of Sutton coll.)

62.   Although the route had been singled, the line on the left of this northward view was retained as a long siding. The gates had been controlled by a wheel in the signal box, which is marked S.B. on the map. It had a 30-lever frame and was replaced in 1930 by a small hut containing a ground frame. (R.S.Carpenter coll.)

63.   On the right is the short goods loop and shed. The yard closed on 1st August 1967. The photograph is from 1964. Coals of different types were both loaded and unloaded here, the latter being for local domestic use. (R.K.Blencowe)

64.   A passing loop was re-established in September 1997 and DFR trains were regular visitors from 12th October 2003, but passengers could not alight. This southward view is from 28th September 2005. (A.Pace)

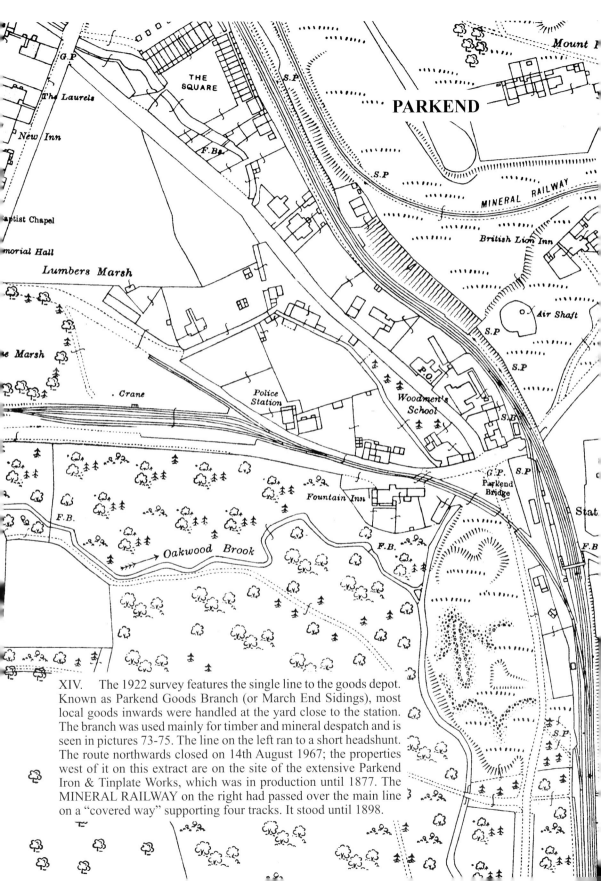

G.P

The Laurels

New Inn

THE
SQUARE

S.P

PARKEND

Mount

Baptist Chapel

F.B.

S.P

Memorial Hall

Lumbers Marsh

MINERAL RAILWAY

British Lion Inn

Marsh

Crane

Police
Station

P.O.

Woodmen's
School

Air Shaft

S.P

S.P

S.B

G.P. S.P
Parkend
Bridge

Fountain Inn

F.B.

Stat

F.B

F.B.

Oakwood Brook

S.P

XIV.   The 1922 survey features the single line to the goods depot.
Known as Parkend Goods Branch (or March End Sidings), most
local goods inwards were handled at the yard close to the station.
The branch was used mainly for timber and mineral despatch and is
seen in pictures 73-75. The line on the left ran to a short headshunt.
The route northwards closed on 14th August 1967; the properties
west of it on this extract are on the site of the extensive Parkend
Iron & Tinplate Works, which was in production until 1877. The
MINERAL RAILWAY on the right had passed over the main line
on a "covered way" supporting four tracks. It stood until 1898.

65.　　An indifferent postcard is worth including as it shows the full range of buildings. The goods shed (left) had been moved from the end of the goods branch in 1897. Beyond the crossing, there had been a siding for an iron furnace around 1870. (M.J.Stretton coll.)

66.   A postcard view east has the goods shed and yard nearest. This traffic ceased on 1st August 1967. The signal box is on the left and it closed on 2nd October of that year. It had a 27-lever frame. (I.A.Pope coll.)

67.   Views of passenger trains prior to their withdrawal in 1929 are rare. This one is from 1922, when road competition was developing. A Cinderford-Lydney train waits with four-wheeled coaches evident and a van at the front. (H.J.Patterson Rutherford/R.S.Carpenter coll.)

68.   Looking north in 1964, we see the goods branch curving left and the goods yard centre. The gate posts are evident, but the gate is open and thus unclear. The footbridge was doubly useful, as the station served as the junction for some Coleford trains and it linked footpaths. The tall building in the background had been the Iron Works engine house; the other structures had gone in 1890. (R.K.Blencowe)

69.   Looking in the opposite direction from the footbridge in 1964, we note the loading gauge. The gate just beyond it was across the siding of Cruwys & Hoborough, which was in use until 1906. (R.K.Blencowe)

70.   Parkend had been the base of the Dean Forest Railway from 1971 until 1978 and it used the old goods shed (right), which dated from 1897. The first steaming day here was on 23rd October 1971, when Peckett 0-4-0ST *Uskmouth* ran with a brake van. Seen undergoing a steam test on 28th March 1976 is ex-GWR 2-6-2T no. 5541. It had arrived from Barry via BR on 11th October 1972 and subsequently became a star attraction, but was withdrawn in 2004. (T.Heavyside)

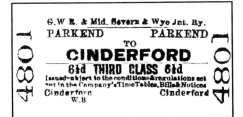

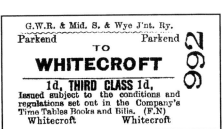

71.   A northward panorama from the footbridge seen in picture 68 shows a station-in-waiting on 26th May 2001. On the platform is a replica S&WR building and to the left is the early goods shed. The level crossing had been reinstated in October 1997 and a run-round loop was created. (P.G.Barnes)

72.   New level crossing gates were fitted in October 2004, a DMU ran on 27th December 2005 and regular passenger service recommenced on 25th March 2006, after a gap of 77 years. Hunslet 0-6-0ST *Jessie* was recorded on 27th May of that year. It was on the DFR from 1980 until 2007. Double track extended 200yds northwards by 2008, so that visiting trains would be accommodated, and further growth was anticipated. (M.Dart)

PARKEND GOODS BRANCH

73.	This was the second level crossing on the short branch and was opposite the Fountain Inn (left), which is marked on the map. The end of the line is in the background of this 1966 photograph. (R.K.Blencowe)

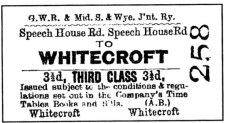

74.   Nearer to the wharf in May 1964 is 0-6-0PT no. 9619 and on the former is the crane, which is annotated on the map and also shown in the next picture. (R.K.Blencowe)

75.   No. D9555 was shunting on 31st March 1967. The Oakwood Tramroad had once run from the top of the wharf direct to Milkwall. The wharf carried six tramway tracks, ending at three turntables. The line from Lydney closed to regular traffic on 7th May 1976, but a railtour ran in March 1980 and it was used monthly until July 1981 to maintain the right of way for possible opencast coal traffic. (J.M.Tolson/F.Hornby)

NORTH OF PARKEND

76.   Travellers Rest signal box was ¼ mile from Parkend and it was named after a local inn (it was eventually renamed "The Railway"). This northward view includes a class 2021 0-6-0PT about to leave the up loop. There were two loops on the down side, at the far end of which was Coleford Junction. There was a line to Parkend Royal Colliery behind the box; the track was in use until 1928. There was another short branch nearby to Parkend Stone Works until 1932. (Rev. D.A.Tipper/I.A.Pope coll.)

Coleford Branch

77.   A southward view at the north end of the loops has the remnant of the colliery siding on the left and the Coleford branch on the right, climbing at 1 in 30. On the extreme right is a bank of sand covering the siding intended to catch any runaways. This and the next picture date from April 1946. (L.E.Copeland/Wild Swan Publications)

78.   Moving a little further north, we see the convergence of the lines at Coleford Junction. Coleford trains were detached here from Cinderford services or simply reversed here. There had been a platform in the left foreground for use by workmen in about 1889-1906. (L.E.Copeland/Wild Swan Publications)

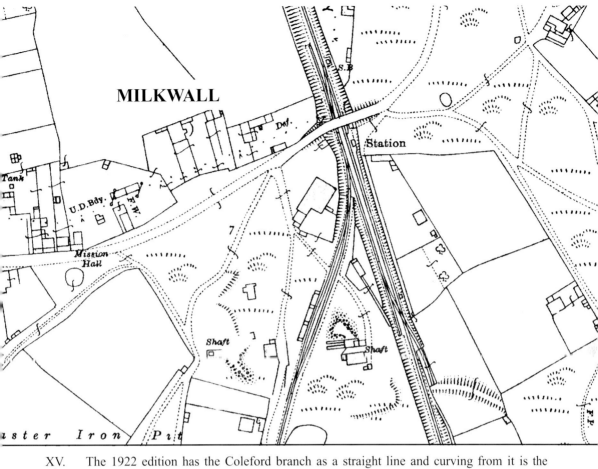

MILKWALL

XV.   The 1922 edition has the Coleford branch as a straight line and curving from it is the Sling branch, which served the Easter Iron Ore Mining Company, Dun Pit Iron Mines, New Ham Pit, British Pit (Clearwell Iron Mine), Sling Pit and Forest of Dean Stone Firms Ltd. at different times. Similarly, the Coleford Junction - Milkwall route had sidings for Darkhill Colliery and Brickworks, Hopewell Colliery, Venus Colliery and Flutterhill Brickworks.

79.   The standard S&WR building is seen in June 1922, but it was destroyed by fire in June 1923. The Sling branch curves off the loop on the left. (H.J.Patterson Rutherford/R.S.Carpenter coll.)

80.　　The replacement building was less flammable, but served passengers for only six years. It is seen from the Sling branch in 1965; this climbed at 1 in 40 most of its ½ mile length. (R.K.Blencowe)

81.　　The entire loop is evident as no. 8745 runs down the 1 in 31 gradient in April 1965 with stone from Whitecliff Quarry. This was on the GWR branch to Coleford, the remainder of which closed in 1917. (R.K.Blencowe)

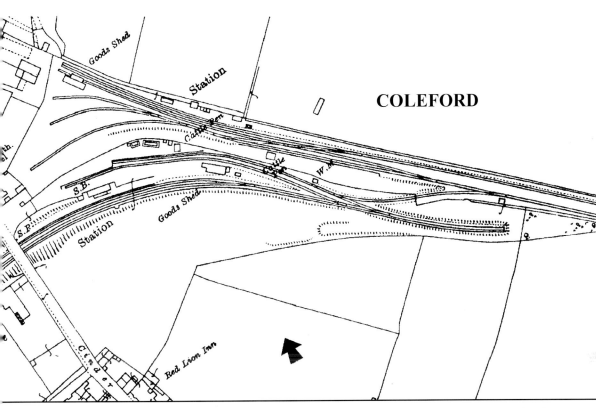

COLEFORD

XVI. The line from Milkwall is on the right of this 1921 map, and the former S&WR station is at the top. The 1883 GWR route from Monmouth and its terminus are on the left.

82. The goods shed is viewed through the loading gauge and on the left is the church tower, which is in the market place in the town centre. Evident is the original building, which was destroyed by fire on 20th July 1918. As at Milkwall, it followed complaints about inadequate accommodation. (M.J.Stretton coll.)

83.   A new building was not completed until 1924; the temporary one can be seen beyond it.
The water tower had replaced a timber structure in 1895. The crossing had been used by passengers
to and from the GWR station until 1903; it closed in 1917. (R.S.Carpenter coll.)

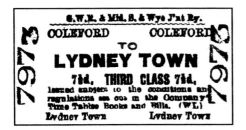

84.   There was no connection between the two railways here until December 1885. The map shows the indirect link passing through a gate, which is illustrated. The arrangement required no signalling. The GWR headshunt is on the right. A direct connection was provided on 21st October 1951. (R.Dagley-Morris/I.A.Pope coll.)

85.   All traffic was transferred from the goods shed in the distance to the one on the left in 1918. The latter became the home of the Coleford GWR Museum in 1988. The ex-S&WR cattle pen is in the foreground. (P.J.Garland/R.S.Carpenter coll.)

86.   A railtour stands at the disused platform on 13th May 1961, while the steps and handrails of the autocoach are extended for photographers to alight. The cattle dock is on the right. (H.C.Casserley)

> **Views of the GWR side of the station can be found in pictures 69-76 in our *Branch Lines around Monmouth*.**

87.   The view has changed little as class 14 no. D9555 shunts on 31st March 1967. Goods traffic ceased on 1st August of that year. This class served the locality well in the final years of traffic. (J.M.Tolson/F.Hornby)

➔ XVII. We return to the main route, with the terminus at Coleford lower left and the one at Cinderford on the right. The map continues from no. VII, after picture 27. The top left part of that extract joins the lower centre part of this one. On the boundary was Bicslade Siding, which served a tramroad that ran to a quarry near Purples Hill between 1812 and 1947. Speech House Road is marked as B4226 and runs across the lower part of the map. The station is below the word "Cannop". "Colliery" above it refers to Cannop Colliery, which had a siding from 1907 until 1960. West of it was the Wimberry Tramroad. The Lydbrook branch is left of centre.

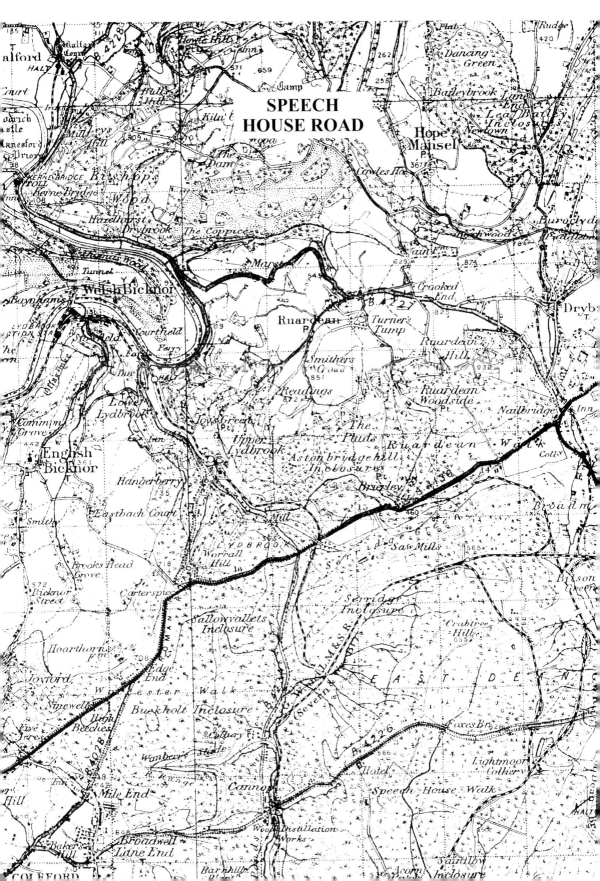

SPEECH HOUSE ROAD

88. Bicslade Siding was a little over one mile north of Parkend and the loop was on the west side of the line. It is occupied by no. 2044 in the Summer of 1948. Both stone and coal was loaded here, but the tramroad was lifted in 1952 and was probably the last in the district. (Rev. D.A.Tipper/I.A.Pope coll.)

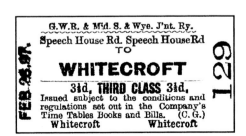

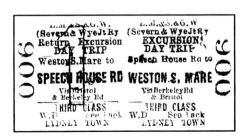

89. An explanation of "Speech House" is necessary. Its location is shown as "Hotel", east of Cannop on map XVII. It was built in 1676 as a hunting lodge for King Charles II and became the administrative centre for the Royal Forest. The Verderers Court is now the hotel dining room and is still complete with traditional fittings. The Court can meet every 40 days, but now usually gathers quarterly. The Crown still offers the ancient fees of "one doe and a buck", but there are no claimants at present. The Court of Mine Law has also met here in times past. (V.Mitchell)

90. Looking north in 1922 we see the end of a massive timber frame, which was probably used for wartime timber traffic. Beyond it is a standard 5-ton crane. (H.J.Patterson Rutherford/ R.S.Carpenter coll.)

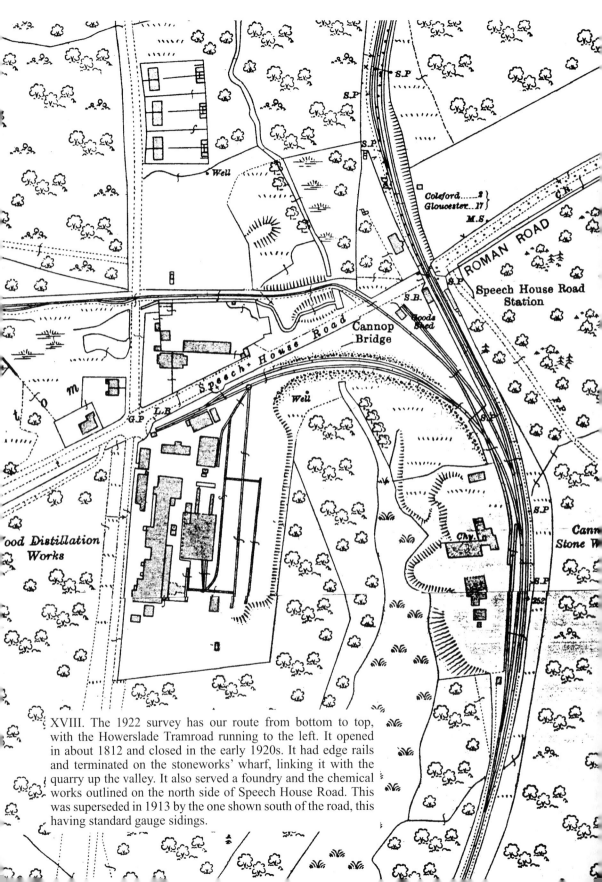

S.P

S.P

S.P

Well

Coleford....2
Gloucester...17

M.S.

G.N.

ROMAN ROAD

S.P

Speech House Road
Station

S.B.

Goods
Shed

Speech · House · Road

Cannop
Bridge

Well

G.P   L.B

m

O

S.P

S.P

Chy.

Cann
Stone W

252

ood Distillation
Works

XVIII. The 1922 survey has our route from bottom to top, with the Howerslade Tramroad running to the left. It opened in about 1812 and closed in the early 1920s. It had edge rails and terminated on the stoneworks' wharf, linking it with the quarry up the valley. It also served a foundry and the chemical works outlined on the north side of Speech House Road. This was superseded in 1913 by the one shown south of the road, this having standard gauge sidings.

91. The signals are for two single lines running north, the left one for Cannop Colliery and the right for Cinderford. A scissors crossover was installed north of the level crossing in 1912, but it is not shown on the map. A half-cab is running south in May 1950 on economy track. (R.G.Nelson/T.Walsh)

92. The other up starting signals are halting the REC "Severn Venturer" on 15th April 1956. The train was hauled by 0-6-0PT no. 1625. There had been a staff of five in the 1920s at this station. (Stations UK)

93.　　The Wood Distillation Works produced charcoal and chemicals vital for the manufacture of explosives. It was operated by the Ministry of Munitions from 1914 to 1919 and was subsequently used intermittently by various firms, finally closing in June 1972. No. 1627 is on its siding in April 1961. (Rev. D.A.Tipper/I.A.Pope coll.)

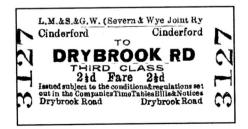

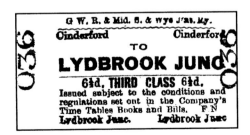

94.   Wagons stand in the goods yard, which closed on 12th August 1963. The siding to the works (left) soon followed. The lines northwards closed on 21st November 1960. The photograph is from September 1960. (R.Dagley-Morris/I.A.Pope coll.)

95.   The stationmaster once had a good view of his empire from the 1888 residence in the background of this 1963 picture. The 1908 signal box had 46 levers in its frame and closed on 12th August 1963. A local trespasser is departing. (T.Gough/M.J.Stretton coll.)

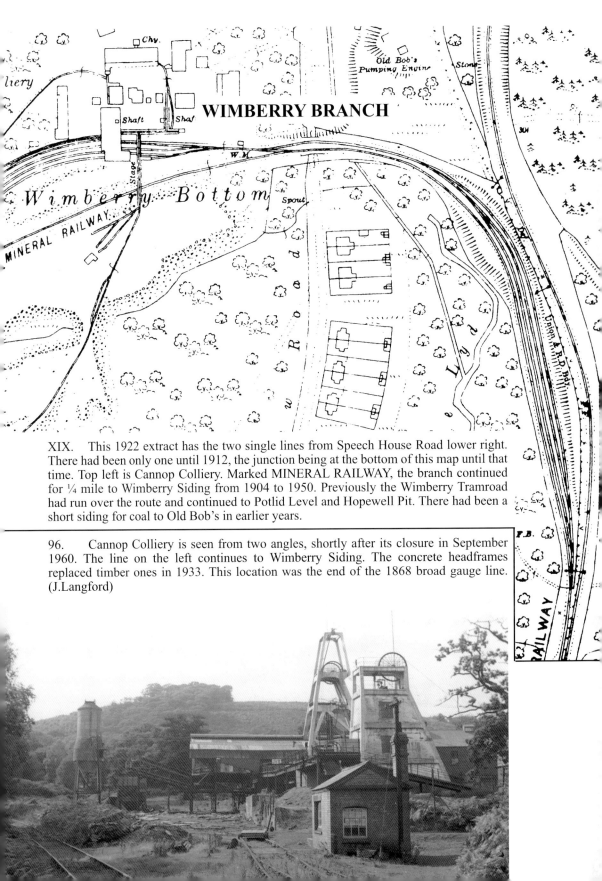

WIMBERRY BRANCH

XIX. This 1922 extract has the two single lines from Speech House Road lower right. There had been only one until 1912, the junction being at the bottom of this map until that time. Top left is Cannop Colliery. Marked MINERAL RAILWAY, the branch continued for ¼ mile to Wimberry Siding from 1904 to 1950. Previously the Wimberry Tramroad had run over the route and continued to Potlid Level and Hopewell Pit. There had been a short siding for coal to Old Bob's in earlier years.

96. Cannop Colliery is seen from two angles, shortly after its closure in September 1960. The line on the left continues to Wimberry Siding. The concrete headframes replaced timber ones in 1933. This location was the end of the 1868 broad gauge line. (J.Langford)

97. Cannop Colliery had a siding from January 1907, but the pit did not open until 1912. It had incorporated the Old Furnace Level and the 1897 Wimberry Colliery. On the left is a pneumatic dry cleaning plant, which separated the dust from the small coal. (J.Langford)

98. Hopewell Pit reproduction headgear was recorded on 1st June 2001, the site having opened as a museum in 1997. Coal mining is still undertaken at a few small mines operated by Freeminers. The centuries old mining rights entitle any male born within the hundred of St Briavels, aged 21 or more and who has worked for a year and a day in a mine to register as a Freeminer with the chance of being granted a "gale" of coal (or ore). However, there is now no maternity hospital in the area. Hopewell Colliery offers underground tours.
(P.G.Barnes)

Lydbrook Branch
SERRIDGE JUNCTION

XX.   The junction for the Lydbrook line is on the left and the route to Cinderford is on the right on this 1933 map at 6ins to 1 mile. Speech House itself is close to the lower border (left) and north of it was Speech House Colliery until 1909. It opened in 1874 and was known as Great Western Colliery for some time. The siding diverged on the embankment shown on the right of map XIX and climbed at 1 in 30. The Mineral Loop curves south at Drybrook Road, having last been seen on map XII at Tufts Junction. Inset and continuing from the opposite page, is one of the collieries on the Mineral Loop. The sidings at Trafalgar Colliery (top left) were in use from 1890 until 1926. The continuation opposite has Cinderford top right and its earlier station northwest of it. Lower right is the GWR line to Newnham. Bilson Road platform (1876-78) had been near the footpath which crosses the line west of Cinderford Old Station. Across the top is the GW&MJR direct line to the town, this opening on 2nd July 1900.

99.   A northward panorama has the Lydbrook Junction route plus two loop lines on the left. On the right is a timber loading siding, which was disused by about 1952. Pit props were a common commodity. There had been a platform here until 1879, but only down trains called at it in its final years, owing to the gradient being 1 in 40. (L.E.Copeland/Wild Swan Publications)

100.   There was a rare opportunity to see the 23-lever signal box on 23rd September 1950, when ex-GWR railcar no. 7 paused on a railtour. The box closed on 12th December 1951. (H.C.Casserley)

NORTH OF SERRIDGE JUNCTION

101.   First was Speculation Colliery Siding, followed by Mierystock Sidings for Arthur & Edward Colliery, Brierley Siding and Waterloo Pit. This is the second and is seen in the 1930s. (I.A.Pope coll.)

102.   Empty wagons were hauled by rope to the loading lines under the screens (centre). The shed on the left housed the winding engine and the one on the right was for wagon repairs. The line was open from the south until 1960; closure northwards was in 1956. (I.A.Pope coll.)

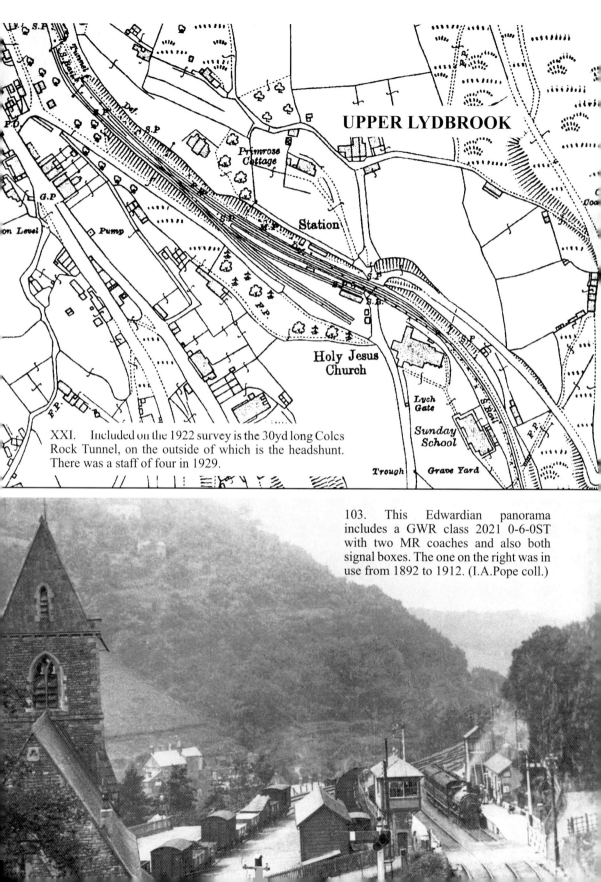

UPPER LYDBROOK

Primrose
Cottage

Station

Holy Jesus
Church

Lych
Gate

Sunday
School

Trough   Grave Yard

XXI.   Included on the 1922 survey is the 30yd long Colcs Rock Tunnel, on the outside of which is the headshunt. There was a staff of four in 1929.

103.   This Edwardian panorama includes a GWR class 2021 0-6-0ST with two MR coaches and also both signal boxes. The one on the right was in use from 1892 to 1912. (I.A.Pope coll.)

104.   The station gardens complemented the beautiful environment, seen in 1923. Trains running north from this stop descended on the valley side at 1 in 50. (I.A.Pope coll.)

105.   A 1922 southward view includes mining activity on the hillside and a classical cast iron urinal. The signal box had 28 levers and was downgraded to a ground frame in 1929, when passenger service ceased. Behind it is the goods shed; the yard closed on 30th January 1956. (H.J.Patterson Rutherford/R.S.Carpenter coll.)

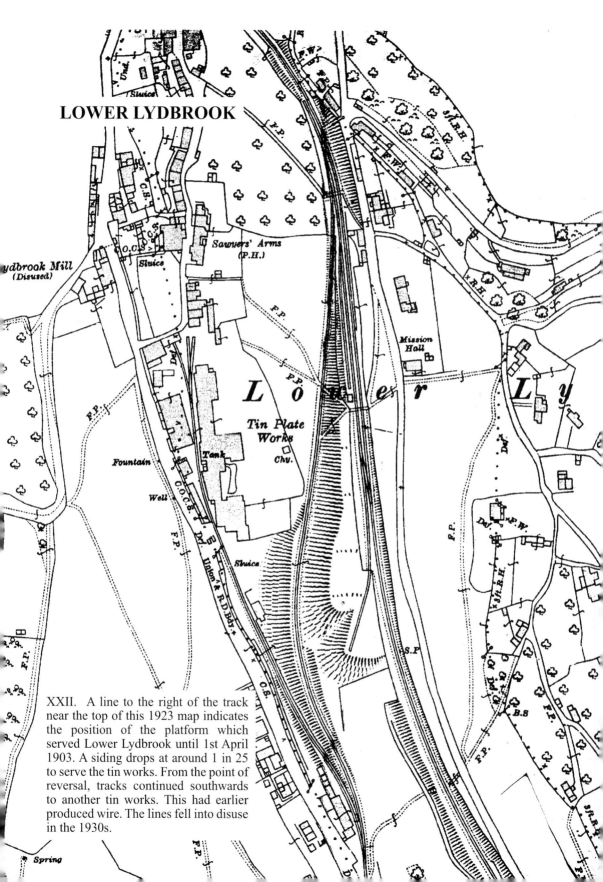

LOWER LYDBROOK

Lydbrook Mill
(Disused)

Sawyers' Arms
(P.H.)

Mission
Hall

Fountain

Tin Plate
Works

Tank

Chy.

Well

L o w e r   L y

Sluice

Spring

XXII. A line to the right of the track near the top of this 1923 map indicates the position of the platform which served Lower Lydbrook until 1st April 1903. A siding drops at around 1 in 25 to serve the tin works. From the point of reversal, tracks continued southwards to another tin works. This had earlier produced wire. The lines fell into disuse in the 1930s.

106. The foundation stone of this viaduct was laid in November 1872 and the structure was completed in August 1874. The line down to the works is on the left and the platform is on the right. (I.A.Pope coll.)

107. There was a speed limit of 6mph on the structure, which was reduced to 5 in 1911. The outer spans were 120ft in length and the centre one was 150ft. The complete viaduct was listed as 187yds long. (R.E.Davies/I.A.Pope coll.)

108.   The end was nigh on 6th August 1965, around nine years after the last train had rumbled over the spans. No longer could it be used as an illegal footpath. North of this structure was Bicknor Siding, from 1888. It had a cattle pen and a goods shed. (G.Adams/M.J.Stretton coll.)

LYDBROOK JUNCTION

XXIII. The 1883 Ross & Monmouth Railway's route is from right to left on this 1922 edition. Lower is the 1884 line from Serridge Junction, which closed as far as Mierystock Siding on 30th January 1956. On the left are three exchange sidings. There was a staff of six here in 1929.

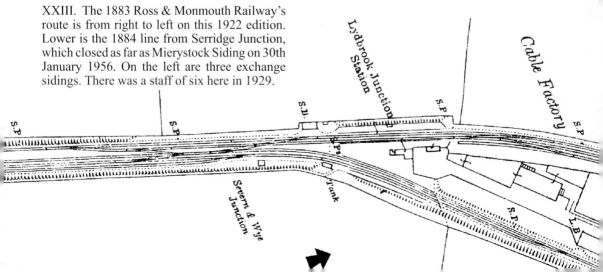

109.   This 1922 view towards the junction is from the platform commonly used by trains from Cinderford. The one on the left had been seldom used. The signal box dated from 1908 and had 43 levers. (H.J.Patterson Rutherford/R.S.Carpenter coll.)

Other views can be found in pictures 59-64 in our
Branch Lines around Monmouth.

110.   The "Last train from Monmouth to Ross" stopped for photographs on its approach to the station on 4th January 1959. Public goods traffic continued from Ross-on-Wye until 2nd November 1964 and the AEI cable works was served until 31st October 1965. (S.Rickard/J&J coll.)

DRYBROOK ROAD

111.   The station is at the top of map XX (left of centre, after picture 98) and was at the northern end of the Mineral Loop, seen on the right of this 1948 photograph. There is only one platform, the other track being a goods loop. There is also a loop on the mineral line. The signal box had 35 levers and became a ground frame in May 1927. (L.E.Copeland/Wild Swan Publications)

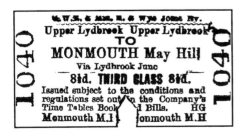

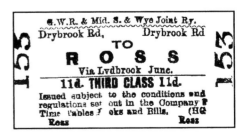

Mineral Loop

112.   The sidings are listed from north to south, with the years of operation of the tramway and/or railway. Through running ceased in 1942. New Fancy Pit was an important source of traffic on the route from 1898 to 1944. Its location is shown near the top of map VII. (I.A.Pope coll.)

Crumpmeadow Colliery	1829-1929
Woorgreen Colliery	1903-1912
Lightmoor Colliery	1823-1940
Acorn Patch Depot	1943-1953
New Fancy Pit	1840-1944

113.   New Fancy Pit was owned by Parkend Deep Navigation Collieries Ltd, hence the Parkend wagons on the approach lines. (I.A.Pope coll.)

NORTH OF CINDERFORD

114.   This is Cinderford Junction which is top right on map XX, shown after picture no. 98. Our route is straight and the line to Newnham curves left in this October 1946 view. The curve opened on 6th April 1908 and the straight line closed on 9th December 1951. (L.E.Copeland/Wild Swan Publications)

115.   Nearing the terminus on 23rd September 1950 on its journey from Newnham is 0-4-2T no. 1409. The fixed distant was for Cinderford Junction, where there was an eleven-lever signal box in 1908-51. There had been a headshunt under the bridge until 1941. (H.C.Casserley)

CINDERFORD

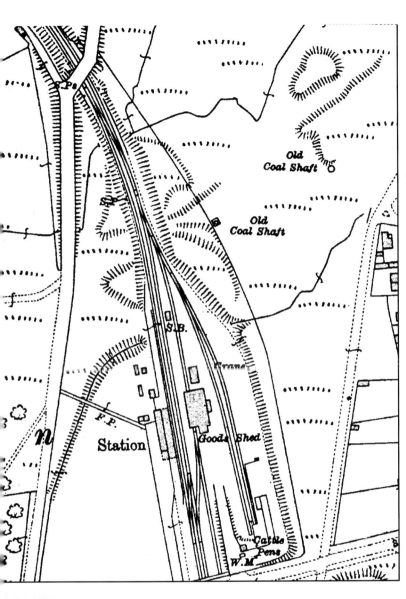

Old
Coal Shaft

Old
Coal Shaft

S.B.

Crane

F.P.

Station

Goods Shed

Cattle
Pens

W.M.

XXIV. The 1922 map shows the station to be on the fringe of habitation. The crane was listed as of six-ton capacity in 1938. The final full year of the service from Lydney (1928) had two trains to Lydbrook Junction reversing here.

116.   The new joint station was much nearer the town centre and was basically of GWR design. The approaching locomotive is a GWR class 2021 0-6-0ST. The weigh house is on the right. (I.A.Pope coll.)

117.   A view towards the buffers has the Railway Hotel in the background and the 16-lever signal box centre. This closed on 17th May 1927, being replaced by ground frames at the ends of the loop. (I.A.Pope coll.)

118.   The autocoach is about to depart empty to Lydney, having worked here as the 7.40pm from Gloucester on 9th August 1947. The sign was double-sided when installed in 1900. There was a local service north to Drybrook until 1930. (SLS coll.)

119.   The reason for the roof being longer than the building is now apparent. The cantilevered design avoids supports obstructing the platform. The 0-6-0PT is about to propel its train to Gloucester on 25th May 1957. The town's population was 6918 in 1961. (F.Hornby)

120.   The 4.8pm to Gloucester was hauled by 0-6-0PT no. 3740 on 15th October 1958; passenger service ceased on 3rd November following. Freight traffic continued until 1st August 1967, but parcels only to 3rd January 1966. (SLS coll.)

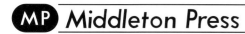

Middleton Press

Easebourne Lane, Midhurst, West Sussex.
GU29 9AZ   Tel:01730 813169

www.middletonpress.co.uk   email:info@middletonpress.co.uk
A-978 0 906520 B-978 1 873793 C-978 1 901706 D-978 1 904474 E-978 1 906008

EVOLVING THE ULTIMATE RAIL ENCYCLOPEDIA

OOP Out of print at time of printing - Please check availability   BROCHURE AVAILABLE SHOWING NEW TITLES